21st
Century
Skills Library

ROAD TO RECOVERY

CALIFORNIA CONDOR

Susan H. Gray

Cherry Lake Publishing
Ann Arbor, Michigan

Published in the United States of America by Cherry Lake Publishing
Ann Arbor, Michigan
www.cherrylakepublishing.com

Content Adviser: Kathy Sullivan, Condor Coordinator, Arizona Game
and Fish Department

Photo Credits: Cover and page 1, ©Rick & Nora Bowers/Alamy; pages 4 and 12,
©Charles Melton/Alamy; page 6, ©Papilio/Alamy; page 8, ©AlanHaynes.com/Alamy;
pages 10 and 28, ©Condor 36, used under license from Shutterstock, Inc.; page 14,
©Pixel 8/Alamy; page 17, ©AP Photo/Ben Margot, Pool; page 18, ©AP Photo/Los
Angeles Zoo; page 20, ©Stock Connection Distribution/Alamy; page 22, ©iStockphoto.
com/xelf; page 25, ©AP Photo/San Diego Wild Animal Park; page 26, ©Kim Worrell,
used under license from Shutterstock, Inc.

Map by XNR Productions Inc.

Library of Congress Cataloging-in-Publication Data
Gray, Susan H.
California condor / Susan H. Gray.
    p. cm.—(Road to recovery)
ISBN-13: 978-1-60279-318-7
ISBN-10: 1-60279-318-2
1. California condor—Juvenile literature. I. Title. II. Series.
QL696.C53G73 2009
598.9'2—dc22   2008024228

Cherry Lake Publishing would like to acknowledge the work of
The Partnership for 21st Century Skills.
Please visit www.21stcenturyskills.org for more information.

TABLE OF CONTENTS

CHAPTER ONE

A Long Wait   4

CHAPTER TWO

The Condor's Life   6

CHAPTER THREE

The Disappearing Condor   12

CHAPTER FOUR

Signs of Hope   17

CHAPTER FIVE

Some Good News   25

Map   29

Glossary   30

For More Information   31

Index   32

About the Author   32

A LONG WAIT

Condors choose nesting sites that are safe from predators and severe weather. A cave in a cliff is one common location.

It is day 56 for the pair of California condors (*Gymnogyps californianus*). Exactly 8 weeks ago, the female laid 1 large, pale blue-green egg. Since then, she and her mate have taken turns keeping it warm. On stormy days, they both remained at the nest. On clear, bright days, one always stayed with the egg while the other flew out alone to search for food.

Suddenly, they hear a faint pecking sound coming from the egg. The pecking stops for a moment, then starts up again. This continues all day, through the night, and into the next day. Pecking. Silence. Pecking. Silence. The condors stay with their egg, keeping it warm and safe. Finally, a light gray, featherless head pokes through a crack in the shell. A condor chick is ready to face the world.

Unlike many other birds, condor pairs do not build a nest together. Instead, they select a **cavity** in the side of a cliff or rocky mountain. Such a spot is safe from most **predators**. Not just any cavity will do. The nesting cavity must have a level floor and plenty of space for the adults and their young. The birds do not add leaves or twigs to their home, and the female lays her egg right on the floor. Why do you think it's important for the floor to be level?

CHAPTER TWO

THE CONDOR'S LIFE

Condors have no feathers on their heads and necks.

The California condor is the largest North American bird. Adults weigh up to 22 pounds (10 kilograms) and have a wingspan of up to 9.5 feet (2.9 meters).

Except for a few places on its body, an adult condor is covered with black feathers. There are triangular patches of white feathers on the underside of its wings. The head and neck are completely featherless, and they are covered with pink, yellow, or orange skin.

Between January and April, females lay a single large egg. For the next 8 weeks, the parents take turns keeping the egg warm. Finally, the baby condor begins to peck its way free. Hatching is slow and may take up to a week.

The adult birds share the job of feeding their chick. One parent remains at the nest while the other parent flies off in search of food. Parents do not return to the nest with food in their beaks. Instead, they swallow the food and fly back to the nest. Then they **regurgitate** the food for their young.

When birds swallow their food, it goes into a chamber in the throat called the crop. There, it is moistened and softened. Next, the food moves on to other digestive organs that break it down into smaller and smaller pieces. Birds such as the condor will often keep food in their crops. They store it there while they fly back to their nests. At the nest, they regurgitate the food for their young to eat.

Birds that do this are often those that **forage** over great distances. By storing food in the crop, these birds do not have to carry it in their beaks. Can you think of some other advantages to storing food in the crop while flying?

Young condors have dark heads. Their heads become lighter when they are 3 to 4 years old.

A condor chick begins to explore when it is about 2 or 3 months old. It makes short trips, hopping around the nesting area. The young bird begins to fly when it is 6 or 7 months old. But it doesn't leave the nesting cavity for good. It will remain close to home for about 1 year. Female birds lay 1 egg every 2 years. That leaves the parents free to care for each chick for a long period of time.

Young California condors aren't ready to have chicks of their own when they leave their nests. Males begin courting females about 5 to 7 years later. During courtship, the males stand in front of the females, spread their magnificent wings, and slowly turn in circles. When condors choose a mate, the pair remains together for life. If one partner dies, the other will choose a new mate.

California condors spend much of their time soaring in the air, searching for food, gathering at feeding areas, and cleaning their feathers. When soaring, they take advantage of columns of warm air rising from Earth's surface. These columns are called **thermals.** They

When California condors take to the air, they spend most of their time soaring with their wings outspread. They seldom flap their wings unless they are taking off or landing. With their enormous wingspans, they need plenty of space for those takeoffs and landings. Do you think this is the reason that condors prefer to feed in open areas? Why or why not?

Condors may fly for hours in search of a meal.

form when hot air rises from warm areas on the ground. Condors spread their wings and "ride the thermals" by circling in an upward spiral. While circling, the condors search for food. They have excellent eyesight and can spot their meals from high in the sky.

Condors are **scavengers**. They do not hunt living animals. Instead, they eat animals that have already died.

They feed on the **carcasses** of deer, cattle, sheep, and other mammals. Condors that live close to the ocean eat dead sea lions and whales. Often, several condors gather to feed on the same animal, making hissing and snorting sounds as they eat.

California condors are surprisingly tidy animals. After feeding, they scrub their heads against grass, shrubs, or rocks. This helps remove any blood or tissue that stuck to their heads while feeding. Because their heads and necks are featherless, they are easier to clean after eating. The birds also bathe often and may spend hours smoothing and drying their feathers.

21st Century Content

Scavengers such as the California condor play an important role as nature's "clean-up crew." They spot decaying animals and devour them, leaving little behind. Condors are built perfectly for this job. Their keen eyesight helps them spot carcasses from far away. Their featherless heads and necks are easy to clean after feeding. And their strong **immune systems** keep them from becoming sick after eating rotten food.

CHAPTER THREE

THE DISAPPEARING CONDOR

An adult condor and a young condor perch on a rock.

California condors have lived in North America for thousands of years. In fact, scientists have found condor **fossils** that are about 100,000 years old. The fossils were discovered in western North America, in Florida, and in New York.

In the early 1800s, American explorers reported seeing the birds in a narrow strip of land stretching from British

Columbia, Canada, to Baja California, Mexico. The 19th and 20th centuries brought many changes to that strip of land. Throughout the 1800s, people seeking gold, land, jobs, and new lives moved to the American West. They dug for gold, cleared land, started farms and ranches, and built cities. The human population increased and cities grew larger as development continued in the 20th century.

All of this growth affected the condors' natural home. Their **habitat** was quickly disappearing. Other factors were working against the condors, too. Ranchers often used animals baited with poison to control predators. Some condors ate the poisoned animals and died. People also shot the birds.

Some condors died from lead poisoning. The lead came from their food. When people shot wolves, deer, coyotes, or other animals, they often left the carcasses to

DDT is a chemical that can be sprayed on plants to kill harmful insects. The United States banned the use of DDT in 1972.

rot. Condors would swoop in and feast on the meat. As they ate, they swallowed bullet fragments and lead shotgun pellets. The lead remained in their bodies, causing them to become sick or to die.

Condors often took in more than bullet fragments and lead when they ate. Sometimes they swallowed metal objects, pieces of plastic, and even glass. These objects often cut the birds' throat tissues or blocked their digestive systems. Parents sometimes regurgitated these objects for their young. A chick that swallowed one of these objects would suffer a painful death.

In the mid-20th century, condors faced another type of poison. It has a long chemical name, but is called DDT for short. People sprayed DDT on their crops and gardens to kill harmful insects. Animals that ate those plants took in a lot of DDT. Many of them died. Condors that fed on those dead animals took the poison into their own bodies. The DDT may have caused some condors to die. The DDT may also have had an effect on condor eggs. Some studies show that it caused females to lay eggs with unusually thin shells. The eggs were fragile and broke easily. DDT may have caused fewer and fewer condors to hatch each year.

Habitat loss, shootings, strange objects in their food, and poisons all took their toll on the California condors. No one has the exact numbers, but by 1939 there may have been fewer than 150 condors left on Earth. By 1967, there were probably fewer than 60 birds left in the wild. By 1982, they numbered less than 25. The California condor was headed for **extinction**.

CHAPTER FOUR

SIGNS OF HOPE

Two young condors are released into the wild.

As far back as 1901, California had a law to protect the condor. The law said that people needed special permission to kill or collect certain birds, including condors.

Experts handle a California condor. Zoos and wildlife organizations have played an important role in helping to increase the condor population.

Unfortunately, officials did little to enforce the law. Many people ignored it.

In 1937, the United States Forest Service created a condor **sanctuary** in southern California. It was a large area that included condor nesting spots and water. About 10 years later, the Forest Service created a second sanctuary. Both were meant to be places where condors could eat, lay their eggs, and live in safety. People were not allowed to build homes, start businesses, or hunt there. No one could even enter the sanctuaries without permission. But the sanctuaries were not enough to save the birds. Condor numbers continued to drop.

In 1973, the United States government created the **Endangered Species** Act. This law was intended to protect plants and animals that were in danger of dying out. It said that land where those species could live safely should be set aside. It urged states to work together to

To help condors survive, people must respect the birds and their habitats while enjoying outdoor activities.

protect endangered species. It also said that people who harm them should be punished. The government also created a list of endangered species. The California condor was on it from the very start.

Many people hoped the new law would save the California condor. They expected to see the condor population increase. Unfortunately, this did not happen. Condor numbers fell even more.

In the 1980s, experts took some big steps toward saving the condor. They began to trap some birds so they could mate and lay their eggs in **captivity**. About this time, scientists learned something important about condor mothers. If their single egg disappeared, the mothers might lay a second egg. Scientists realized they could "encourage" the mothers to lay second, and even third, eggs in the same year. They did this by

Saving an endangered species takes a lot of time, hard work, and planning. Many experts must come together and share their knowledge. They must decide the best way to help the species survive.

The California Condor Recovery Team formed with this goal in mind. The team included people from zoos, universities, the United States Fish and Wildlife Service, the California Department of Fish and Game, and other organizations. They were experts on condor behavior, food, habitats, eggs, and young.

This team met many times to discuss ways to help the condor. Sometimes, team members had big disagreements, but they didn't give up. Instead, they continued to meet and work out their problems. In time, they created a plan to help the California condor survive.

Power lines can be dangerous for California condors and other birds.

carefully removing each new egg and keeping it warm in an incubator until the chicks hatched.

Despite these efforts, the condor population remained small. Scientists were learning better ways to keep the birds alive in captivity, but condors in the wild continued to die. So experts finally decided that it was best to trap the remaining condors in the wild and place them in captivity. In 1987, they captured the last wild condor.

Scientists cared for the birds for the next few years. The population began to increase. In 1989, the number of California condors rose above 30—the first time it had been that high in years. In 1992, the number was close to 60, and scientists released a few birds back into the wild in California.

As the captive population grew, scientists continued releasing condors into the wild. They hoped the wild

How do scientists teach condors to avoid power poles? They give captive birds a choice of different perches. The birds can choose to perch on power poles or on natural landings, such as rocks or dead trees. When they land on the poles, the birds receive a mild electrical shock. They soon learn that it is unpleasant to land on the power poles. Do you think it is mean to treat the birds this way? Why or why not?

population would begin to increase on its own. But problems soon arose. A few of the released birds died. Some collided with power lines because they couldn't see them. Power lines in areas where condors are found are now marked.

Scientists also taught captive birds to avoid power poles. The training worked. When trained condors were released, they stayed away from power poles.

Unfortunately, birds continued to die from poisoning. Scientists found that lead was still a problem. Now, wildlife experts are asking hunters to use bullets and other ammunition made of different materials, such as copper. In Arizona, hunters' organizations have been encouraging their members to switch. Now, many hunters prefer the new ammunition. As a result, fewer condors are being exposed to lead.

CHAPTER FIVE

SOME GOOD NEWS

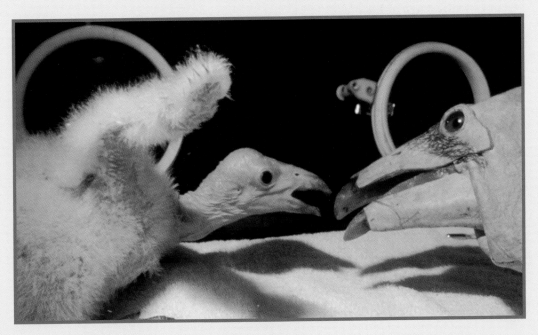

Scientists try to recreate natural conditions for captive condors. This condor chick is being fed with a hand puppet that looks like an adult condor.

Since 1987, when the last wild condor was captured, the population has slowly increased. By the spring of 2008, there were nearly 300 California condors. About half were in captivity, and the other half were soaring freely in California, Arizona, and Mexico.

Scientists now follow the lives of condors in the wild. They watch for males doing courtship activities. They keep

Condors released into the wild have number tags and special devices that help scientists track them.

an eye out for young birds just learning to fly. They want to make sure that California condors in the wild are doing well and are raising chicks. The real success stories are the condor families that are surviving and growing in their natural homes.

At the lowest point, there were only 22 California condors in existence. Now they number in the hundreds.

While this is great news, the work cannot stop. No habitat is completely safe. Foreign objects still show up in the animals that condors eat. Lead poisoning remains a problem. The California condor is still an endangered species.

The goal of the California Condor Recovery Team is to have the bird moved from the list of endangered species to the list of threatened species. Threatened species are those that have a better chance of survival, but whose populations are still small. To become listed as threatened, there must be at least two California condor populations in the wild, and one in captivity. Each population must have at least 150 birds

The recovery plan for the California condor includes much more than just raising and releasing birds. The plan says it is necessary to protect the birds' habitat and to educate the public about the condors' needs. Why is it so important for people to know about California condors?

In 2008, there were about 60 condors living in Arizona.

and be self-sustaining. Scientists hope to reach this goal at some point in the near future.

Today, both the captive and wild populations are increasing, and the species is slowly recovering. The California condor has certainly come a long way over the last 20 years.

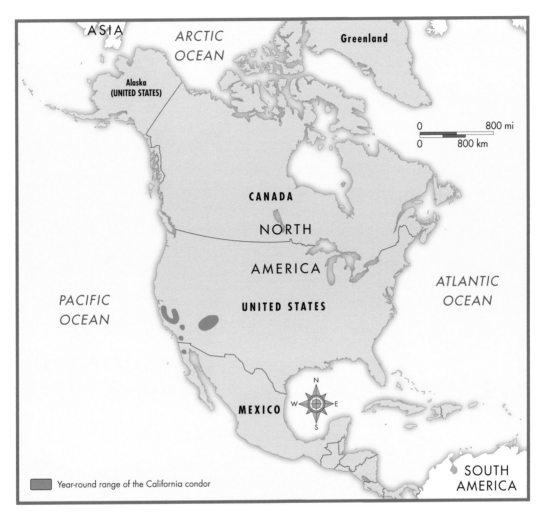

This map shows where California condors live in the wild.

Glossary

captivity (kap-TIH-vuh-tee) the state of being kept within certain boundaries

carcasses (KAR-kuhss-ez) the bodies of dead animals

cavity (KAV-uh-tee) a hole or hollow space in something

endangered species (en-DAYN-jurd SPEE-sheez) a group of similar plants or animals that are in danger of dying out completely

extinction (ek-STINGKT-shuhn) the state of having died out

forage (FOR-ij) to search for food

fossils (FOSS-uhlz) bones, beaks, eggshells, or other remains left by a dead plant or animal

habitat (HAB-uh-tat) the place where a plant or animal normally lives and grows

immune systems (ih-MYOON SISS-tuhmz) systems of organs and tissues that protect animal and human bodies against infections and disease

predators (PRED-uh-turz) animals that hunt and eat other animals

regurgitate (ree-GUR-juh-tate) to throw up food that has not been digested

sanctuary (SANGK-choo-er-ee) a protected place of safety

scavengers (SKAV-uhn-jurz) animals that do not hunt, but eat animals that have already died

thermals (THUR-muhlz) rising air currents

FOR MORE INFORMATION

Books

Becker, John E. *The California Condor*. San Diego: KidHaven Press, 2004.

Imbriaco, Alison. *The California Condor: Help Save This Endangered Species!* Berkeley Heights, NJ: MyReportLinks.com Books, 2008.

Miller-Schroeder, Patricia, and Susan Ring. *California Condors*. Chicago: Raintree Publishing, 2004.

Web Sites

California Condor Conservation
www.cacondorconservation.org
For information about the California condor recovery program, including updates on the condor populations

National Geographic: California Condor
animals.nationalgeographic.com/animals/birds/california-condor.html
To hear California condor sounds and learn more about them

San Diego Zoo: California Condor
www.sandiegozoo.org/animalbytes/t-condor.html
To see pictures of California condors and learn some fun facts about them

INDEX

bathing, 11

California Condor
  Recovery Team, 21, 27
captivity, 21–22, 23,
  25, 27, 28
chicks, 5, 7, 8, 9, 15,
  21, 26
cleaning, 11
courtship. *See* mating.
crops, 7, 15

DDT, 15
digestive systems, 7, 15

education, 27
eggs, 4–5, 7, 8, 15,
  19, 20, 21
Endangered Species
  Act, 19
extinction, 16
eyesight, 10, 11

feathers, 5, 6–7, 9, 11
females, 4, 5, 7, 8, 9, 15

flying, 7, 8, 10, 26
food, 5, 7, 9, 10–11,
  13–14, 16, 21, 27
foraging, 7
fossils, 12

habitats, 13, 16, 21,
  27, 29
hatching, 5, 7, 15, 21
humans, 12–13, 15,
  16, 17, 19, 20

immune systems, 11

laws, 16, 17, 19
lead poisoning, 13, 14,
  24, 27

males, 9, 25
mating, 9, 20, 24

nests, 4, 5–6, 8, 9

perches, 23
poisoning, 13–14, 15,
  16, 24, 27

poisons, 13, 16
population, 16, 19–20,
  20–21, 22, 23–24,
  25, 26, 27–28
power poles, 23
predators, 13

recovery plans, 21, 27
regurgitation, 7, 15

sanctuaries, 18–19
scavenging, 10–11
size, 6

thermals, 9–10
threatened species, 27

United States Forest
  Service, 18–19

weight, 6
wingspan, 6, 9

ABOUT THE AUTHOR

Susan H. Gray has a master's degree in zoology. She has written more than 90 science and reference books for children, and especially loves writing about animals. Susan also likes to garden and play the piano. She lives in Cabot, Arkansas, with her husband, Michael, and many pets.